WEEKLY WR READER®
EARLY LEARNING LIBRARY

I'm Ready for Math

I Know Shapes

Reading consultant: Susan Nations, M.Ed.,
author, literacy coach,
and consultant in literacy education

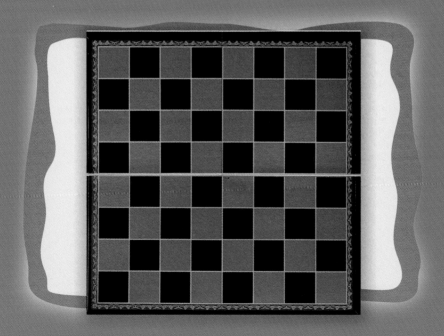

Please visit our web site at: www.earlyliteracy.cc
For a free color catalog describing Weekly Reader® Early Learning Library's list
of high-quality books, call 1-877-445-5824 (USA) or 1-800-387-3178 (Canada).
Weekly Reader® Early Learning Library's fax: (414) 336-0164.

Library of Congress Cataloging-in-Publication Data

I know shapes.
  p. cm. – (I'm ready for math)
 ISBN 0-8368-6477-8 (lib. bdg.)
 ISBN 0-8368-6482-4 (softcover)
 1. Geometry–Juvenile literature. I. Title.
 (Firm) II. Series.
QA445.5.I46   2006
516'.15–dc22   2005030761

This edition first published in 2006 by
Weekly Reader® Early Learning Library
A Member of the WRC Media Family of Companies
330 West Olive Street, Suite 100
Milwaukee, WI 53212 USA

Editor: Dorothy L. Gibbs
Art direction: Tammy West
Cover design and page layout: Kami Strunsee
Photographer: Gregg Andersen

Printed in the United States of America

1 2 3 4 5 6 7 8 9 10 09 08 07 06

Note to Educators and Parents

Learning to read is one of the most exciting and challenging things young children do. Among other skills, they are beginning to match the spoken word to print and learn directionality and print conventions. Books that are appropriate for emergent readers will incorporate many of these conventions while also being appealing and entertaining.

The books in the *I'm Ready for Math* series are designed to support young readers in the earliest stages of literacy. They will love looking at the full color photographs while also being challenged to think about and develop early math concepts. This integration allows young children to maximize their learning as they see how thoughts and ideas connect across content areas.

In addition to serving as wonderful picture books in schools, libraries, and homes, this series is specifically intended to be read within instructional small groups. The small group setting enables the teacher or other adult to provide scaffolding that will boost the reader's efforts. Children and adults alike will find these books supportive, engaging, and fun!

—Susan Nations, M.Ed., author, literacy coach,
and consultant in literacy development

circle

4

A **circle** is round.

side

side  side

side

rectangle

A **rectangle** has
2 long sides and
2 short sides.

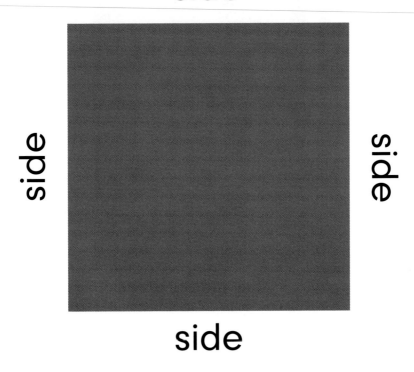

side

side

side

side

square

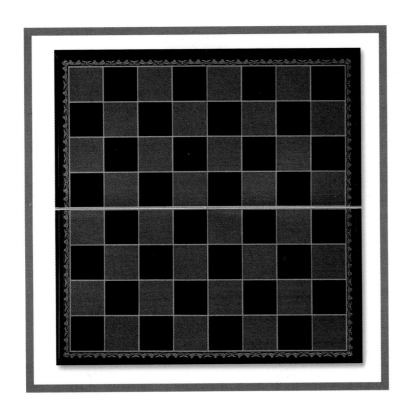

A **square** has 4
sides that are all
the same size.

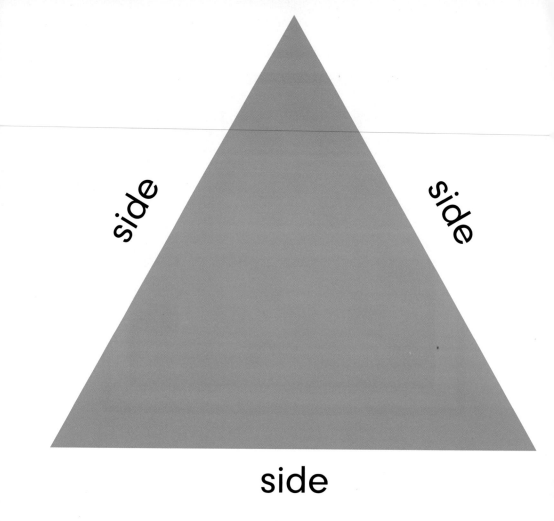

triangle

A **triangle**
has 3 sides.

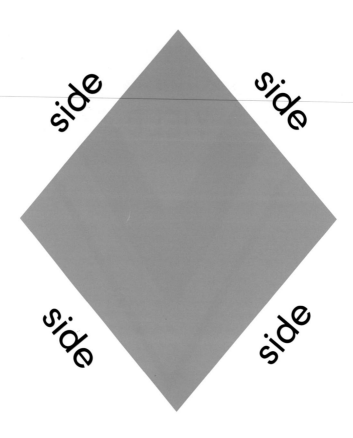

side side

side side

diamond

A **diamond** has
4 sides. It stands on
one of its points.

oval

An **oval** looks like
a long circle.

Can you name these shapes?

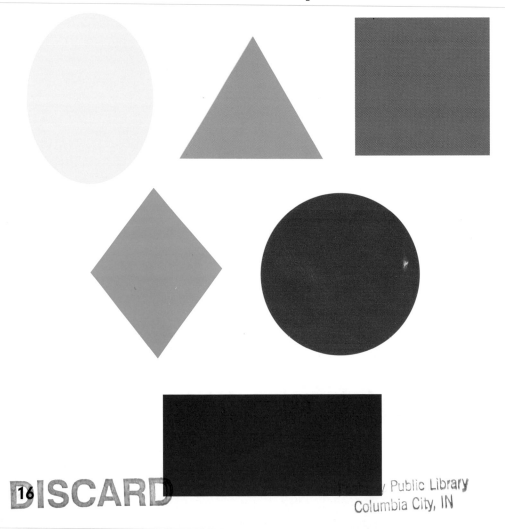